THE GIBSON FAMILY GENEALOGY

By

Katherine Fletcher

GIBSON FAMILY TREE

The Gibson family has a unique mix including Melungeon, African, Portuguese and Native America.

According to the documents I found on Melungeon, I discovered a few facts relevant to the family tree. There apparently was only one or a few Portuguese connections. Mostly these are Indian lines and mixed white lines. Melungeon was a term given to them by white people as an insult and derogatory word. There is a mix of some African, Indian and white.

The Goings / Goins which are in your tree are believed to be from Africa. The Gibsons, Sextons, Collins are all known to be mixed Indian and white families who settled on Newman's Ridge in Tennessee (Sneedville).

These Indian lines go back to Cherokee, Shawnee, Iroquois, Delaware and Pohawatan. It also includes Sapponi Indians which are believed to be part of the Tuscarora Indians.

Records indicate that the Gibson and Collins names were stolen names from white settlers. Mullins seems to be a white line, Denham is the Portuguese line and Goins is the African line.

Many of these people claim to be Portuguese maybe so they would be less discriminated against.   They had more rights being listed as white Portuguese than Africans or Indians.

<u>Generation One</u>

Living Person

GENERATION TWO

Wilburn Isaac Gibson   (1953-2013)
and living person

Wilburn was born in Scott County,
VA.   Here is his obituary and
findagrave information.

Wilburn Issac "Wimp" Gibson, 60,
Gate City, VA passed away,
Thursday, February 28, 2013 at
Wellmont Holston Valley Medical
Center.

Wimp was born in Scott County, VA
on February 24, 1953 to the late
Junior and Alma Peters Gibson.   In
addition to his parents, his infant
brothers preceded him in death.

GENERATION THREE

Lewis Cesco Gibson Junior
(1920-2012) and Alma Catherine
Peters (1922-)

Lewis also known as Junior was born
in Scott County, VA and died in
Kingsport, Sullivan County, TN.
In the 1930 census, attached to the
tree show that he is listed as a Negro
(black).   His parents were from
Virginia and he had lots of siblings.
Junior was 10 years old in the 1930
census.

Lewis has a WWII Young Men's
Draft Card which I attached to his
documents. This document says he
is a dark complexion, brown eye
color, black hair color, 6 ft. 1 in
height and in 1941 was living in Gate
City, Scott County, VA.   He was a
Private in the Army.

His find a grave biography states that was a Reverend and died at 91 years old.   He died at Indiana Path Hospital and was of the Holiness Faith.   His parents are listed as Cisco and Mary. He was preceded in death by five sisters and two brothers.   He was married to his wife Monnie for 33 years.   Alma is listed as white and born in West Virginia.

Alma's parents are Randolph Harvey Peters and Ella Peters.   Their fathers are brothers, and they share the same grandparents.   They are second cousins.   The Peters family is from Germany.   Ella's mother is Sarah Rosenbaum.

His children:

Harless Gibson - Dungannon, Virginia

Wilburn "Wimp" Gibson and wife

Judy of Gate City, VA

Roy (Ross) Gibson of Fairview, Virginia

Tim Gibson and wife Sherry of Weber City, VA

four stepchildren who he raised and loved as his own.

The stepchildren were

Penny and David Bevins from Bristol, BA

Kim and Jeff Necessary, Nashville, TN

Randall and Myra Vanzant - Blackwater Virginia

Matthew and Sherry Vanzant - Blackwater, VA.

pic of Junior Gibson found on findagrave.com biography page.

He divorced his wife Alma in 1979 and the legal cause of divorce is listed as one year continuous and uninterrupted separation.

GENERATION FOUR

Lewis Francesco "Cesco" Gibson 1882-1969 and Mary Lane (1887-1986)

He fought in WWI

In the Virginia death records, Lewis Cesco is listed as a white man.   He died of a heart attack and also had prostate cancer.

Mary Lane's parents are Nathaniel Lane and Katherine Gibson.   The Lane family includes Quakers from Maryland. They originally came from London, England.   The Lane family includes surnames of McClellan, Conn, Corbin, Burrage, Tydings, Sparrow and others.

Here is a pic of Mary Lane

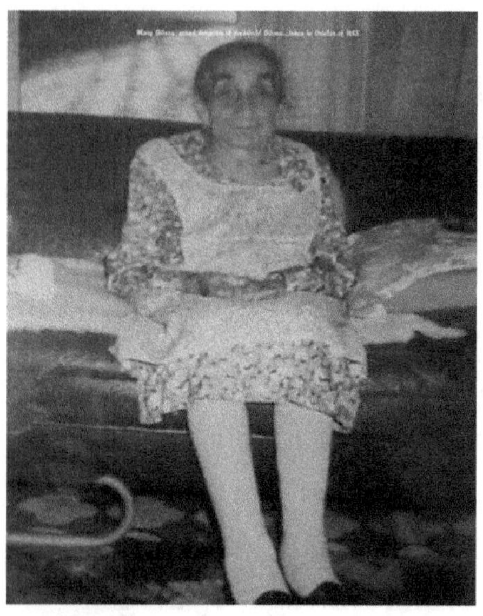

The Katherine Gibson line goes back to Archibald Gibson and Roseanne Sexton.   This Sexton line includes her grandfather Andrew and great grandfather Barlett Sexton and Catherine Gallion.   The Gallion line is the Indian line of this family.

Catherine Gallion m. Bartlett Sexton.

Catherine's parents are Young

Gallion, a Cherokee and April, also a Cherokee. This line goes really far back to Pohowtan Virginia Natives.

GENERATION FIVE

Isaac C. Gibson (1849-1909) and Anna J. Gibson(1851)

Isaac was born in Scott, Virginia and married Anna.

He is listed as White in the census.

Annie's parents are Hiram Gibson and Lydia Moore.   Her Gibson line hooks up with the other Gibson lines in this tree.   These two are related.

GENERATION SIX

John Gibson (1805-) and Tanza Sexton (1805-1870)

John Gibson 1805 Virginia and died 1891 in Nashville, TN.

Tanza Sexton was born Scott, Virginia.   The Sexton family comes from Limerick, Ireland and immigrated to Hampden Massachusetts in the middle 1600s. This line also includes a long Spencer line from England that immigrated to Connecticut in the mid 1600's. Another line is this family is the Crockett family also from Ireland. The Sexton family is also listed as a Indian family. Some of the Sexton family were known to be Cherokee Indians.

Here is a picture of John and Tanza Sexton.

GENERATION SEVEN

John William Gibson 1770-1850 and Frances Rowe 1770-

John was born in Scott County, VA and died in Pike County, KY.

GENERATION EIGHT

James Thomas Gibson (1750-1835
and Sarah Roark 1750-1810

James was born in Halifax, VA and
died in Whitley, Kentucky.

Sarah Roark was born in Surry, NC
and died in Knox, Whitley County,
KY.   Her parents are Barnabas Roark

and Sarah Summers.   The Roark family comes from Ireland.

<u>GENERATION NINE</u>

Gideon Gibson (1716-1781) and Mary Anne Browne 1706-1754

Gideon was born in Lancaster, Virginia and died Hickory Grove Plantation, near Sandy Bluff, SC. He was a soldier in the Revolutionary War.

The first record in South Carolina regarding Gideon Gibson is found in the entry at an assembly meeting where it was announced that "several free colored men with their white wives" recently come from Virginia with intentions of settling on the Santee. [SC Common House Journal 1731-33, pgs. 724-725, entry date 28 June 1731]

The head of this family was summoned to Charleston where he

met with the governor. After which Gov. Johnson reported back to the House of Commons about that interview, the following was recorded in the official records of the province:

They stated the Gibson's were not negroes or slaves but free people. That Gideon and his father are free men. He was a carpenter by trade and was married to a white woman, had some land and seven negroe slaves.

Mary Ann was born Isle of Wight, Virginia and died in Edgecombe, SC.

GENERATION TEN

John Jordan Gibson (1670-1733) and Eliza Willcocks (1670-1792)

John was born in Middlesex, Virginia and died in Old, South Carolina.

Eliza came from England to Louisa, Virginia.

*** I think the further line of Gideon is an unknown Indian, black and/or Portuguese.   Remember they took their name from white settlers.   But we know that Gideon is a very dark skinned man.

GENERATION ELEVEN

John Gibson (1630-1697) and Dorothy Haverd (1632)

John was born in Tynemouth, Northumberland England and died in Middlesex, Virginia.   Dorothy was also from Northumberland England.

SOURCES AND MORE INFORMATION TO READ

This doc is a great breakdown of the various Melungeon lines from Kentucky, Newman's Ridge, TN and Scott County, VA.
http://historical-melungeons.com/wash.html

http://historical-melungeons.com/history.html

Goings family - African?
http://www.historical-melungeons.com/meltree.html

http://www.dnaexplain.com/Publications/PDFs/MelungeonsMulti-EthnicPeopleFinal.pdf

http://www.dnaexplain.com/Publications/PDFs/MelungeonsMulti-EthnicPeopleFinal.pdf

http://www.historical-melungeons.co

m/gibsontl.html

ancestry.com

wikipedia.com

www.ingramcontent.com/pod-product-compliance
Lightning Source LLC
Chambersburg PA
CBHW072333270726
48658CB00016B/2399